READ WITH Biff, Chip & Kipper

Oxford Reading Tree

Helping Your Child to Read

All the practical help you need!

Annemarie Young and Kate Rut

OXFORD

Contents

Learning to read

This book shows you how to help your child from an early age so that learning to read is successful and enjoyable for you both. Children whose parents read with them at home and talk about books have a huge advantage at school and with reading.

Read with Biff, Chip and Kipper books feature the familiar and much-loved characters from the *Oxford Reading Tree*, which is used in 80% of primary schools. The series is based on the *Oxford Reading Tree* and reflects how reading is taught at school.

How to make your child a successful reader

From babyhood onwards, you can help your child to enjoy books, to understand how books work, and to learn what it means to be a 'reader'. This book gives you practical tips and ideas for each of the stages of a child's early reading development, including playing games, doing activities and reading a wide range of books together.

How can the *Read with Biff, Chip and Kipper* books help my child?

This fun, innovative series is designed to give beginner readers a good start. The stories are full of humour and always have a satisfying ending. There are two strands in the series: First Stories introduce young readers to common words and everyday language; Phonics books enable children to practise their letters and sounds just as they do at school. There are six graded levels in each strand, providing gradual progression and vocabulary repetition.

Tips and ideas

Every book in the series includes practical tips for you, and fun activities for your child, which will help to develop their reading skills.

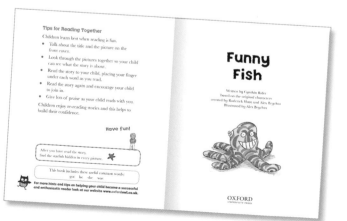

Level 1   Getting ready to read

ORT Level 1-1+

Age 4-5

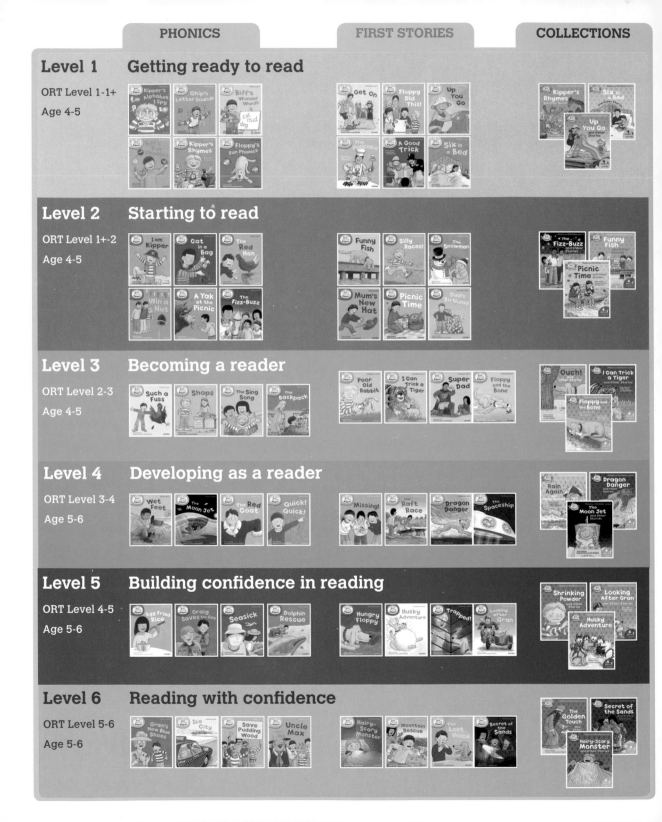

Level 2   Starting to read

ORT Level 1+-2

Age 4-5

Level 3   Becoming a reader

ORT Level 2-3

Age 4-5

Level 4   Developing as a reader

ORT Level 3-4

Age 5-6

Level 5   Building confidence in reading

ORT Level 4-5

Age 5-6

Level 6   Reading with confidence

ORT Level 5-6

Age 5-6

How does your child learn to read at school?

Schools use a range of methods to teach children to read. The main one currently used is called 'synthetic phonics'.

In nursery and the early months of school, there is emphasis on listening to stories and the sounds of the language, including rhyme and rhythm, building up to a focus on synthetic phonics (letter-sound relationships). Children are taught that the letter 's' makes a *sss* sound, as in *sun*; that we say 'a' as in *apple* and 't' as in *tap*. Children can then start to read simple words by blending the sounds together to make a word, e.g. *s-a-t, sat*.

After they have learned the more straightforward letter-sound relationships, they are taught the more complex ones, e.g. that the 'igh' sound as in *high* can also be written as *tried*, *cry* and *nine*.

Sounds are not taught in alphabetical order, instead they are taught in the order best suited to begin blending sounds for reading.

You can listen to the sounds on www.oxfordowl.co.uk. Note that some sounds are pronounced differently according to regional accent so consult your child's teacher for advice if you are unsure.

Tricky words

Because English is not phonically regular, some common, everyday words like *the*, *no* and *said* cannot be read by sounding out. These are sometimes called 'tricky' words. Read these words out to your child and they will soon learn to recognise them by sight. The *Read with Biff, Chip and Kipper Flashcards Word Games* and *Fun with Words* are a fun and effective way to learn and practise tricky words.

7

Choosing the right books for your child

The chart on page 6 provides rough age guidance and *Oxford Reading Tree* stages for each book. However, every child develops at their own pace. The level descriptions below provide more detail to help you decide which level to start with your child. If you are in any doubt ask your child's teacher for guidance.

Level 1: Getting ready to read (4- to 5-year-olds)

is for children who enjoy sharing and talking about books and can:

- listen to a story and retell bits of it
- recognise their own name
- recognise some letter sounds (e.g. some of the sounds in their name)
- pick out patterns and details in pictures
- join in with language play (e.g. songs and nursery rhymes, games like 'I spy' etc)
- match some words (e.g. match *Mum* from a set of cards to the word *Mum* in a sentence)
- sustain concentration for 5–10 minutes.

Level 2: Starting to read (4- to 5-year-olds)

is for children who can:

- read short sentences with simple two and three letter words (e.g. *Mum has a big red bag.*)
- retell a simple story
- recognise 5–10 common tricky words by sight (e.g. *the, and*)
- write their name and a few other common words
- build sentences using familiar words.

Level 3: Becoming a reader (4- to 5-year-olds)

is for children who can:

- read words and sentences containing less common letters, as well as *sh, ch, th* (e.g. *The fox got his fish in the chip shop.*)
- recognise 10–20 common tricky words by sight (e.g. *was, you, they*)

- recognise all the letter sounds at the beginning and end of words
- use some expression when they re-read books.

Level 4: Developing as a reader (5- to 6-year-olds)

is for children who can:

- read some long vowels (e.g. *feet, moon*) and adjacent consonants (e.g. *crash, star*)
- read harder sentences, with less support
- recognise 20–30 common tricky words by sight (e.g. *what, there, some*)
- read words with more syllables and recognise more words in sentences.

Level 5: Building confidence in reading (5- to 6-year-olds)

is for children who can:
- recognise 30–50 common words by sight
- read harder sentences, with less support, and recognise more words in sentences
- can read various spellings of long vowels (e.g. *tried, night, cry* and *nine*)
- recognises all common spelling patterns and knows that many of them can be pronounced in more than one way
- talk about the characters and plot
- begin to read silently.

Level 6: Reading with confidence (5- to 6-year-olds)

is for children who:

- confidently comment on characters, story and plot
- express opinions about what they read
- confidently read different spellings for one sound (e.g. *hair, bear*)
- can read words with common endings (e.g. *turning, turned*) and beginnings (e.g. *return*)
- can read silently
- like to attempt longer books.

Getting ready to read (4- to 5-year-olds)

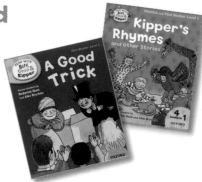

Preparing your child for reading

Sharing books and talking about the pictures with your baby and toddler will increase their language skills and develop their understanding of the world. Even at this early stage, your child will be learning how books work – that they have a front and a back and pages that turn to tell a story. They may like to hold the book and try to turn the pages themselves.

Point to each word on the page as you read to help your child understand how print works – that the marks on the page carry meaning to tell the story. Once they can sustain concentration for five to ten minutes you will be able to help them get ready to start learning to read.

Children need to develop a range of skills, focusing on both the meaning of sentences and shape of a story, and on individual words and phonics.

You can help them by:

- talking about stories and using story language
- helping them develop a knowledge of phonics
- helping them to recognise common words by sight.

In pre-school and Reception, the emphasis is on listening to stories and the sounds of language, including rhyme and rhythm, before introducing phonics.

You can help your child with phonics by playing language games with them: teach them songs and nursery rhymes; invent silly rhymes for them to join in; clap the rhythms of words; help them to think of 'another word that begins with the same sound as…'.

Practical tips

Try to make time to read to and with your child every day. Choose a time when they are not too tired and you are not too busy. Turn off any distractions such as the TV, radio and mobile phone.

- Before you read a story with your child:

  – talk about the title and the pictures on the cover, and look through the book together

  – discuss what you think the story might be about

  – check that your child knows where to start reading and the direction of print across the page.

- Read the story to your child, pointing to the words as you read.

- Re-read the story with your child, encouraging them to join in with repeated patterns.

- Give them lots of praise as they read with you.

Phonic activities

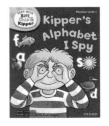

When you have read the story, you can start to draw attention to the words and letters.

Point out the starting sound of a word and then ask them to find another word beginning with the same letter or perhaps to think of a rhyming word.

Ask them to find two words that are the same.

Story activities

When you have finished reading, ask questions like:

- What was your favourite bit?

- Why do you think Floppy joined in?

- What did Kipper take with him?

- What do you like to do with all the family?
  If you know the rhyme, *Ten in a Bed*, you can recite it together.

Level 1: Phonics

The first Phonics book, *Kipper's Alphabet I Spy*, is a fun introduction to each letter of the alphabet and the sound it represents. The second book, *Chip's Letter Sounds*, reinforces and practises letter sounds. *Biff's Wonder Words* introduces simple three letter words such as *sat* and *mud*. *Floppy's Fun Phonics* and *Biff's Fun Phonics* practise reading simple captions and sentences. *Kipper's Rhymes* uses rhyming words to help practise reading simple sentences.

Developing phonic skills

- Encourage your child to recognise letters and rhymes.

- Sing the alphabet song while pointing to letters on a printed letters.

- Recite rhymes they know, like *One, two, three, four, five, Once I caught a fish …*, and get them to supply the missing rhyming word.

- Use modelling clay or playdough to make letter shapes.

- Demonstrate blending by saying the sounds *c–a–t* to read *cat*.

- Use magnetic letters on the fridge and sponge letters in the bath to spell your child's name, and other simple words.

- Find pictures in magazines to make sets of 'Words which begin with …' and make an alphabet scrapbook.

Level 1: First Stories

The Level 1 First Stories are short, amusing stories featuring Biff, Chip, Kipper and Floppy from the *Oxford Reading Tree*. They use simple words and are designed to help build children's confidence at this early stage.

Look through the pictures for each story first, so your child can see what the book is about. Next, read the story to your child, placing your finger under each word as you read. Then read the story again and encourage your child to join in. Re-read the story as many times as your child wants – this helps to build their confidence. Talk about the story together when you have finished.

Get on, Chip.

Chip got on.

Developing reading skills

- Draw attention to special book language, such as *Once upon a time …*

- Encourage your child to retell favourite stories to a friend or grandparent.

- Use the pictures as well as the words to help them understand the whole story.

- Take your child to the library and encourage them to make choices about the books they want to read.

- Enjoy teaching them nursery rhymes and action songs.

- Play *I Spy* on car journeys or listen to audio CDs.

- Read as many books as you can, including re-tellings of traditional tales and fairy stories, alphabet books and even catalogues!

Starting to read
(4- to 5-year-olds)

At this stage your child will be starting to read at school and will probably be bringing books home to practise their skills. But don't stop reading to your child, it is this experience that draws them into reading for enjoyment.

Practical tips

- Keep reading lots of different books *to* your child, and keep bedtime reading special. Most picture books will be too hard for them to read, and it's good for them just to listen to a story and look at the pictures with you.

- Before reading a book together, always talk about the title, the blurb, and the pictures on the cover. Ask your child what they think the book might be about. As you read, point to the words. Let them join in if they want to.

- Read with expression when reading aloud and try different voices for different characters. Get your child to join in with refrains like *They huffed and they puffed!*

- Talk about the stories when you've finished reading together. Ask questions like: *What did you like best? What colours did the snowman wear?*

- Always read a book aloud before you ask your child to read it to you. This gives them the chance to understand the story, and to hear the words and language patterns. Remember, you are not testing your child, knowing what the book is about will help boost their confidence.

Level 2: Phonics

Reading the books together

Each book contains two stories which introduce new letter patterns and help children to practise them.

- Before you start reading, talk about the title and the picture on the cover. Ask: *What do you think the story is about?*

- Look at the focus letter patterns practised in each book. These are listed on the inside front cover.

- Find the pages with the list of words for each story. The focus letter patterns are shown in bold. Say the sounds in each word, then say the word (e.g. *T–e–ss, Tess*).

- Read each story then go back and find the words with those letter patterns. Give your child lots of praise as they read!

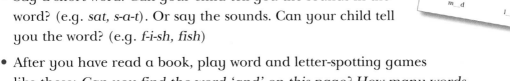

Practising phonic skills

- Find sets of words which begin or end with the same sound.

- Say a short word. Can your child tell you the sounds in the word? (e.g. *sat, s-a-t*). Or say the sounds. Can your child tell you the word? (e.g. *f-i-sh, fish*)

- After you have read a book, play word and letter-spotting games like these: *Can you find the word 'and' on this page? How many words can you find on this page that begin with 't'?*

The sounds and letter patterns practised in Level 2

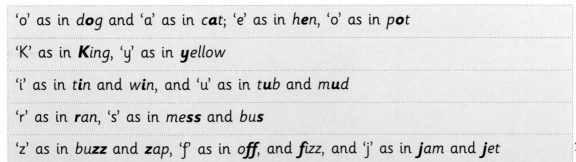

'o' as in *dog* and 'a' as in *cat*; 'e' as in *hen*, 'o' as in *pot*

'K' as in *King*, 'y' as in *yellow*

'i' as in *tin* and *win*, and 'u' as in *tub* and *mud*

'r' as in *ran*, 's' as in *mess* and *bus*

'z' as in *buzz* and *zap*, 'f' as in *off*, and *fizz*, and 'j' as in *jam* and *jet*

Level 2: First Stories

These simple stories help children to practise reading common words and everyday language.

- Before you start reading, talk about the title and the pictures on the cover.

- Look through the pictures together so your child can see what the story is about.

- Read the story to your child, placing your finger under each word as you read.

- Read the story again and encourage your child to join in. Give lots of praise as your child reads with you.

- Have fun finding the objects or creatures hidden in the pictures.

- Discuss the Talk About ideas at the end of each story.

Practising reading skills

Read favourite stories again and again. Children enjoy this and it helps to build their confidence.

Play alliterative games, like 'Annie got an apple, Ben got a bike', or rhyming games.

If your child gets stuck on a word, check first if it can be 'sounded out'. If not, try re-reading the sentence without saying the difficult word. The meaning of the rest of the sentence can often help. If they still can't work out the word, just say it quickly for them and move on.

Useful common words repeated in Level 2

got   he   she   was   had   it   no   go   on   Dad   said
an   ran

Becoming a reader (4- to 5-year-olds)

At this stage your child will be reading simple books with more confidence and developing their reading skills. It's as important as ever to keep a good balance between sharing books together for enjoyment and practising early reading skills.

Practical tips

"Look out!" said Floppy. "There is a bee on your nose."

"Oh no!" said the snake, and she let Floppy go.

- Keep bedtime reading special. Read lots of different books to your child as well as continuing to re-read old favourites.

- Before reading a book together, talk through the story without reading it aloud. Point out any words you think might be difficult and read them out.

- Read the story together, pointing to each word and inviting your child to join in. Give lots of praise as your child reads with you, and help them when necessary.

- Encourage your child to read with expression when re-reading the story.

- Talk about the stories when you've finished reading together. Ask questions like: *What was your favourite bit? Why did the tiger let Floppy go?*

- Introduce paired reading, where you and your child read aloud from the same book together. You can read more quietly as they become more confident.

Level 3: Phonics
Reading the books together

The fox ran off.

"I can soon fix the pen," said Dad.

These stories introduce new letter patterns and help children to practise them.

- Before you start reading, talk about the title and the picture on the cover. Ask: *What do you think the story is about?*

- Look at the focus letter patterns. These are listed on the inside front cover.

- Find the pages with the list of words for each story. The focus letter patterns are shown in bold. Say the sounds in each word, then say the word (e.g. *s–u–ch, such*).

- Read the story then go back and find the words with those letter patterns. Give your child lots of praise as they read!

Practising phonic skills

Point out letters that go together, for example, *th*, *sh*, and chunks of words, such as *-ing*. Help your child to recognise these letter patterns and the sounds they make.

Build a word using magnetic letters and ask your child to make a word that rhymes with it, or is one letter different, or begins or ends with the same letter.

The sounds and letter patterns practised in Level 3

'ch' as in **Ch**ip; 'oo' as in *too*; 'v' as in **V**iv; 'x' as in *fix*

'ck' as in *ba**ck***; 'qu' as in **qu**ick

'sh' as in **sh**op; 'th' as in **th**em

'oy' as in *toy*; 'ing' as in *miss**ing***

'i', 'o' and 'a' as in *ship*, *shop* and *hat*

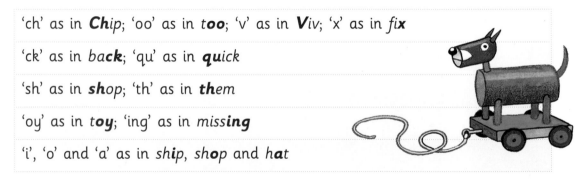

Level 3: First Stories

These stories help your child to practise reading common words and everyday language.

Floppy was dreaming.
He was in the jungle.

- Before you start reading, talk about the title and the picture on the cover. Ask: *What do you think the story is about?*

- Read the story together, pointing to each word and inviting your child to join in.

- Give lots of praise as your child reads with you, and help them when necessary.

- Have fun finding the objects or creatures hidden in the pictures.

- Discuss the Talk About ideas at the end of each story.

- Re-read the story later, encouraging your child to read with you.

Practising reading skills

Clapping out syllables in words and names can help with reading longer words, e.g. *di–no–saur, choc–o–late*. Point out that some words are made up of two smaller words, e.g. *wind* and *mill* together make *windmill*.

If your child gets stuck on a word, try phonics first. If it can't be sounded out, try re-reading the sentence without saying the difficult word. The meaning of the rest of the sentence can often help. If your child still can't work out the word, just say it quickly for them and move on. Return and look at the word more carefully after you have finished reading.

Useful common words repeated in Level 3

said   you   out   the   went   saw   took

look(s)   put   stop

Developing as a reader (5- to 6-year-olds)

At this stage your child will be building on their early reading skills and developing their strategies and confidence. As before, keep a good balance between reading for enjoyment and practising reading skills.

Practical tips

- Continue to read to your child at bedtime.

- Before reading a book together, talk through the story. Point to any words that you think might be difficult and read them out.

- Read the story together, inviting your child to read with you. Give lots of praise and help them when necessary.

- Encourage your child to read with expression when re-reading the story.

- Talk about the story together when you've finished reading.

- Continue paired reading, where you and your child read aloud from the same book together. You can read more quietly as they become more confident.

Level 4: Phonics

Reading the books together

These stories help children practise new letter patterns as well as re-visiting others.

- Before you start reading, talk about the title and the picture on the cover. Ask: *What do you think the story is about?*

- Look at the focus letter patterns. These are listed on the inside front cover.

- Find the pages with the list of words for each story. The focus letter patterns are shown in bold. Say the sounds in each word, then say the word (e.g. *m–oo–n, moon*).

- Read the story then go back and find the words with those letter patterns. Give your child lots of praise as they read!

Practising phonic skills

When you child is reading, help them to look out for whole letter patterns
rather than individual letter sounds (e.g. *sh-ee-p* rather than *s-h-e-e-p*. Write out words they get stuck on, using a different colour for the tricky letter patterns.

Play 'I spy', using words that begin with two consonants, for example, *br, cl, dr, st*; words that end with two consonants, for example, *nd, st, lk*; or words that rhyme.

The sounds and letter patterns practised in Level 4

'ee' as in *fee*t
'i' and 'sh' as in *fish*.
'oo' as in *room* and *rook*
'u' as in *bug* and *Mum*
'oa' as in *coat*
'ck' as in *qui**ck*** and *stu**ck***
'ie' as in *tie* and 'ai' as in *rain*

Level 4: First Stories

Reading the books together

These stories help children practise reading common words and everyday language.

- Before you start reading, talk about the title and the picture on the cover. Ask: *What do you think the story is about?*

- Read the story together, inviting your child to read with you.

- Give your child lots of praise as they read, and help them when necessary.

- Have fun finding the objects or creatures hidden in the pictures.

- Discuss the Talk About ideas at the end of each story.

- Re-read the story later, encouraging your child to read it with you.

Practising reading skills

Draw your child's attention to speech marks, punctuation, sound effects and action words (for example, *BUMP! WHOOSH! CRASH!*).

If your child is still reading 'one-word-at-a-time', let them listen to you reading fluently and with expression and ask them to copy what you do.

WHOOSH! Flames came out of the dragon's mouth.

Floppy hid, but the dragon saw him.

Useful common words repeated in Level 4

saw   said   came   out   she   was   looked   what   help
them   children   went   going

Building confidence in reading (5- to 6-year-olds)

Your child will now be building on their earlier reading skills and developing confidence in reading. The books in both strands of *Read with Biff, Chip and Kipper* are carefully levelled stories full of humour, with a satisfying ending, to keep your child motivated to read whilst developing their confidence and reading skills.

Practical tips

- Even though your child is beginning to read more independently, do keep sharing bedtime stories or information books with them. Choose books together.

- Try sharing a book together – you read one page and your child reads the next. You are showing them what fluent reading sounds like, and if they lose the meaning of the story while concentrating on reading their pages, they can pick up the meaning again while you are reading.

- Talk about the books you read. Ask them to tell you if they don't like a book, and why.

- Get your child to make links between their own experience and how a character responded in the story.

- Your child may be ready to start reading silently. This is harder than it sounds, but as well as reading books aloud together, encourage them to try reading silently when they are re-reading favourite books.

Level 5: Phonics

Reading the books together

These stories help children practise new letter patterns as well as revisiting others.

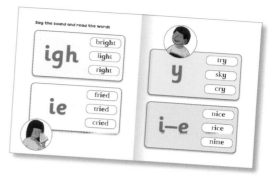

- Before you start reading, talk about the title and the picture on the cover. Ask: *What do you think the story is about?*

- Look at the focus letter patterns. These are listed on the inside front cover.

- Find the pages with the list of words for each story. The focus letter patterns are shown in bold. Say the sounds in each word, then say the word (e.g. *f–r–ie–d, fried*).

- Read the story then go back and find the words with those letter patterns. Give your child lots of praise as they read!

Practising phonic skills

Make jumbled words. For example, cut out letters from a word like *some* and ask your child to rebuild the word.

Ask your child to point out words that have the same sound but are written differently, like the '*igh*' sound as in *tried, night, cry* and *nine*.

The sounds and letter patterns practised in Level 5

'ee' as in *b**ea**ch* and *ch**ee**se*

'igh' as in *tr**ie**d, n**igh**t, cr**y*** and *n**i**ne*

'ai' as in *Cr**ai**g, d**ay**, g**a**me*

'f' as in *dol**ph**in*

'oa' as in *c**oa**t, st**o**ve, J**oe**, sn**ow**, ag**o***

'n' as in *k**n**ight, **n**ot*

'r' as in *w**r**ite, **r**an*

24

Level 5: First Stories

Reading the books together

These stories help children practise reading common words and everyday language.

- Before you start reading, talk about the title and the picture on the cover. Ask: *What do you think the story is about?*

- Read the story together, inviting your child to read as much of it as they can.

- Give your child lots of praise as they read, and help them when necessary.

- Have fun finding the words, objects or creatures hidden in the pictures.

- Discuss the Talk About ideas at the end of each story.

- Re-read the story later, encouraging your child to read as much of it as they can.

Practising reading skills

When your child is reading new words, help them to focus on separate parts of the words rather than individual letter sounds, for example, *butt–er–fly.*

If they get stuck on a word try different ways of helping. Ask them to say the first sound of the word, or break it into chunks, or read the whole sentence again. Focus on the meaning of the word.

When your child re-reads a story ask them to read it with lots of expression. Get them to use different voices for the different characters.

Useful common words repeated in Level 5

thought   must   looking   find   very   must   look(ed)   pull(ed)

suddenly   so   away   fast(er)   must

Reading with confidence (5- to 6-year-olds)

Your child will be building on their reading skills and developing greater confidence in reading. The books in both strands of *Read with Biff, Chip and Kipper* are carefully levelled stories full of humour, with a satisfying ending, to keep your child motivated to read whilst developing their confidence and reading skills.

Practical tips

- Even though your child might like to read independently at this level, don't stop sharing bedtime stories or information books with them. Choose books together and enjoy talking about them. You could take it in turns to read a page.

- Try reading slightly more difficult books to your child. Hearing you read fluently will motivate them to want to read it themselves.

- Talk about the books you read. Let them tell you if they don't like a book, and why. It's OK not to like some books!

- Get your child to make links between their own experience and how a character responded in the story.

- As well as reading books aloud together, encourage your child to read silently and independently.

Level 6: Phonics
Reading the books together

These stories help children practise new letter patterns as well as revisiting others.

- Before you start reading, talk about the title and the picture on the cover. Ask: *What do you think the story is about?*

- Look at the focus letter patterns. These are listed on the inside front cover.

- Find the pages with the list of words for each story. The focus letter patterns are shown **in bold**. Say the sounds in each word, then say the word (e.g. *p–u–dd–i-ng, pudding*).

- Read the story then go back and find the words with those letter patterns. Give your child lots of praise as they read!

Practising phonic skills

Ask your child to find words that look like they should rhyme but don't, for example: *home* and *come*; *do* and *no*. Then ask them to find words which do rhyme even though they look different, for example: *come and sum; there, bear* and *hair*.

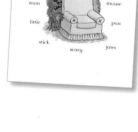

Play games to help your child become familiar with the alternative spellings for sounds. This will help them to speed up their reading, making it more enjoyable.

The letter patterns practised in Level 6

'oo' as in *fl**ew*** and *gl**ue***
'**s**' as in *dre**ss**, nur**se**, pala**ce*** and *c**ity**
'oo' as in *w**oo**d, p**u**dding* and *c**ou**ld*
'le' as in *un**cle***, 'oi' as in *c**oi**n*, 'ow' as in *d**ow**n* and *o**ut***, 'er' as in *dinn**er***, 'oe' as in *t**oe*** and *g**o***
'air' as in *p**air**, there, c**are*** and *b**ear***
'ear' as in *n**ear***, and *h**ere***

Level 6: First Stories
Reading the books together

These stories help children practise reading common words and everyday language.

- Before you start reading, talk about the title and the picture on the cover. Ask: *What do you think the story is about?*

- Read the story together, inviting your child to read as much of it as they can.

- Give your child lots of praise as they read, and help them when necessary.

- Have fun finding the words, objects or creatures hidden in the pictures.

- Discuss the Talk About ideas at the end of each story.

- Re-read the story later, encouraging your child to read as much of it as they can.

Practising reading skills

When your child is reading new words, help them to focus on separate parts of the words rather than individual letter sounds, for example, *sudd–en–ly.*

If they get stuck on a word, ask them to say the first sound of the word, or break it into chunks, or read the whole sentence again. Focus on the meaning of the word.

When your child re-reads a story ask them to read it with lots of expression. Get them to use different voices for the different characters.

Useful common words repeated in Level 6

thought   wasn't   could/couldn't   laughed   something   under

behind   suddenly   shouted   station   climbed/climbing/climber

Questions parents often ask

When should I start reading with my child?

It's never too early. Babies and toddlers enjoy looking at picture books and hearing them read aloud. Chant nursery rhymes, sing songs and share picture books from birth onwards!

Should I teach my child the alphabet?

Yes. Teach the alphabet through songs and games. Encourage your child to learn both letter names and letter sounds by playing games like 'I spy'.

What if my child is more interested in the pictures than the words?

Pictures are an integral part of stories. They give important clues to what is happening. Encourage your child to look closely at the pictures while you read the story to them.

Ask them to make predictions about how a character is feeling by looking at their expression or to think about what might happen next by looking at what is going on in the picture.

What if my child seems to stop making progress?

Don't worry. Children develop at different rates and they always need to consolidate what they are learning before moving on. Continue to re-read familiar books, introduce new books at the same level, play games and always be encouraging. Once they are ready, progress will resume.

What should I do if my child wants the same book over and over again?

Don't discourage them. It's good to have favourite books, and reading familiar stories will give them confidence. Introduce new stories but keep sharing old favourites too.

When and how can I ask my child to start trying to read with me?

Be guided by your child – don't force the pace too early or you risk putting them off. Re-read the advice on the 'Getting ready to read' stage (see page 10). If your child is not yet ready, spend more time reading to them and playing some of the games. If they are asking what words say, they are probably ready to begin to read. Start with a familiar story (e.g. *Goldilocks* or *The Gingerbread Man*) with lots of repeated phrases, like *Who's been eating my porridge?* or *Run, run as fast as you can…* Ask them to join in and place your finger under the words as you read them. The *Read with Biff, Chip and Kipper* stories in Levels 2 and 3 have lots of repeated phrases.

What if my child makes a mistake while they're reading?

Don't stop the flow of the reading unless what they've read doesn't make sense. The meaning is the most important thing in reading in the early stages and accuracy will come.

What should I do if they get stuck on a word?

In the early stages, quietly say the word so that the flow isn't broken. Later you could:

- Get them to sound out the first sound of the word.

- Break the word into chunks (syllables).

- Read the whole sentence again.

- Encourage them to refer to the picture for clues.

- Read on to the end of the sentence and then ask them to guess the word. Focus on the meaning.